Jimmy Carter

A LIFE OF FRIENDSHIP

by Sheila Anderson

Lerner Publications Company • Minneapolis

Photo Acknowledgments

The photographs in this book are used with the permission of: The Jimmy Carter Library, pp. 4, 8, 12, 16, 18, 19, 20, 21, 26; AP Photo, p. 7; © CORBIS, p. 10; © Kevin Fleming/CORBIS, p. 11; courtesy of Georgia Archives, Vanishing Georgia Collection, pp. 13 (FUL0980-85), 14 (SUM0836); Library of Congress, pp. 6,15 (HABS GA, 131-PLAIN, 18-9); p. 15; Andrew Chant/Rex USA, courtesy Everett Collection, p. 22; © Robert Sullivan/ AFP/Getty Images, p. 24, © Bettmann/CORBIS, p. 25.

Front cover: © Wally McNamee/CORBIS

Text copyright © 2008 by Lerner Publishing Group, Inc.

Lerner Publications Company
A division of Lerner Publishing Group, Inc.
241 First Avenue North
Minneapolis, MN 55401 U.S.A.

Website address: www.lernerbooks.com

Words in **bold type** are explained in a glossary on page 31.

Library of Congress Cataloging-in-Publication Data

Anderson, Sheila.
    Jimmy Carter : a life of friendship / by Sheila Anderson.
        p. cm. — (Pull ahead books. Biographies)
    Includes index.
    ISBN 978-0–8225–8585–5 (lib. bdg. : alk. paper)
        1. Carter, Jimmy, 1924–Juvenile literature. 2. Presidents–United States–Biography–
Juvenile literature. I. Title.
    E873.A68 2008
    973.926092–dc22 [B]   2007025130

Manufactured in the United States of America
1 2 3 4 5 6 – JR – 13 12 11 10 09 08

Table of Contents

Jimmy Carter grew up on a farm. He had a horse named Lady and a dog named Sam.

A Boy on the Farm

Jimmy Carter was born on October 1, 1924, in Plains, Georgia. His family lived on a farm. His father grew peanuts and cotton.

Back then, black people and white people did not go to the same schools. They did not sit together on buses.

Black people had to ride at the back of the bus.

Jimmy had two sisters, Gloria *(left)* and Ruth *(right)*.

But Jimmy was a **friendly** boy. He liked everyone, whether they were black or white.

Jimmy married Rosalynn Smith.

A Friend to the Community

After high school, Jimmy went to **college**. Then he married Rosalynn Smith. Soon, they began a family. Jimmy joined the **navy**. Jimmy's family moved a lot because of his work.

Jimmy's father's name was James Earl Carter.

In 1953, Jimmy's father died. Jimmy thought about how his father had helped the **community**.

Jimmy wanted to be like his father. He wanted to be useful to his community.

Jimmy's parents lived in the community of Plains, Georgia.

Jimmy and Rosalynn returned to Georgia.
Jimmy worked on his parents' farm.

Rosalynn and Jimmy moved into this house.

Jimmy *(center)* thanked a group of teachers from Georgia.

He became a leader helping schools and libraries.

Jimmy worked with other leaders to fix the roads.

He joined a club that helped the community.

This dirt road led to the high school in Plains, Georgia.

It raised money to **pave** the dirt roads in town.

In 1977, Jimmy became president of the United States.

A Friend to the World

Jimmy wanted to help his country. He became a leader in his state. Then he ran for president of the United States and won.

Jimmy liked helping Americans.

Jimmy created laws to help people in the United States.

Rosalynn and Jimmy met with the president of Nigeria in 1977.

Jimmy also wanted to help people around the world.

Jimmy met with Anwar Sadat, the president of Egypt.

The countries of Egypt and Israel had been fighting. Jimmy asked the leaders of both countries to come to the United States.

Jimmy talked to them about friendship and peace. They listened to him. They agreed to stop fighting.

The three presidents signed an agreement to stop fighting.

Jimmy wanted to help in other countries too. He flew to Thailand to build new homes after a big storm.

A Friend to the Poor

After four years, Jimmy was done being president. He liked helping people when he was president. He still wanted to help them. He wanted to be a friend to people in need.

Jimmy created the Carter Center. It makes sure people are treated fairly.

Jimmy gives a speech at the Carter Center.

Jimmy and Rosalynn work on a Habitat for Humanity house.

Jimmy also began working for Habitat for Humanity. It builds houses for the poor. Jimmy helped build many houses.

Jimmy Carter

A Life of Friendship

Jimmy Carter has been a friend to many people. His friendship has helped make the world a better place.

JIMMY CARTER TIMELINE

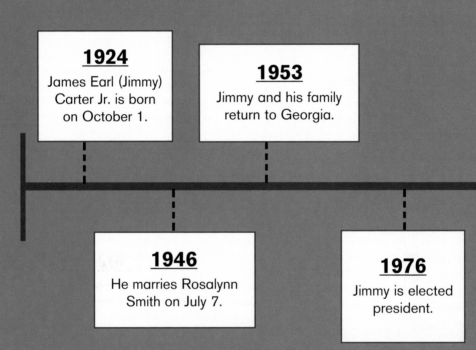

1924
James Earl (Jimmy) Carter Jr. is born on October 1.

1953
Jimmy and his family return to Georgia.

1946
He marries Rosalynn Smith on July 7.

1976
Jimmy is elected president.

1978

He helps the leaders of Israel and Egypt agree to stop fighting.

1999

Jimmy and Rosalynn Carter receive the Presidential Medal of Freedom.

1982

He founds the Carter Center.

2002

Jimmy wins the Nobel Peace Prize.

More about Jimmy Carter

- Jimmy and Rosalynn Carter still build houses for Habitat for Humanity one week every year.

- Jimmy Carter still travels around the world. He helps other countries with **elections** and **human rights**.

- Jimmy Carter has written more than a dozen books.

Websites

The Carter Center
http://www.cartercenter.org

Jimmy Carter and Habitat for Humanity
http://www.habitat.org/how/carter.aspx

Jimmy Carter Library and Museum
http://www.jimmycarterlibrary.org

Jimmy Carter National Historic Site
http://www.nps.gov/jica/

Glossary

college: a school people can go to after high school

community: a place where families live together and feel at home

elections: the act of choosing leaders

friendly: showing good feelings toward others; kind and helpful

human rights: everyone's right to justice, fair treatment, and free speech

navy: a nation's warships, crews, and officers

pave: to cover with a hard surface

Index